ANIMAL MOSAICS

COLORING BOOK

JESSICA MAZURKIEWICZ

DOVER PUBLICATIONS, INC.
MINEOLA, NEW YORK

Artwork created by arranging small objects—usually tiles, pieces of colored glass, or pebbles—into images or patterns can be traced as far back as the third century B.C. The elegantly complex designs typical of mosaics make an ideal addition to Dover Publications' *Creative Haven* series. Providing each colorist with ample opportunity for experimentation with different media and color techniques, the designs in this book feature animals such as the panda bear, flamingo, cat, and more.

Bibliographical Note

Animal Mosaics Coloring Book is a new work,
first published by Dover Publications, Inc., in 2014.

International Standard Book Number

ISBN-13: 978-0-486-78177-8
ISBN-10: 0-486-78177-1

Manufactured in the United States by RR Donnelley
78177105 2016
www.doverpublications.com